THE CAT LADY
OF CONCORD

THE CAT LADY
OF CONCORD

Feline Tales and
Other Animal Stories
of Love and Rescue

FLOY MORWAY

BUNKER HILL PUBLISHING

First published in 2007
by Bunker Hill Publishing Inc.
285 River Road, Piermont
New Hampshire 03779, USA

10 9 8 7 6 5 4 3 2 1

Library of Congress Control Number: 2007926767

ISBN10: 1593730624
ISBN13: 97812593730628

Designed by Louise Millar

Printed in China by Jade Productions Ltd

The organization, **Adopt A Cat**, founded by Floy Morway, 40 years
ago is now known as **Adopt A Cat of Concord** to differentiate
from the many other organizations using her original name.
Any questions or donations can be directed either to the website
www.AdoptaCatofConcord.org
or P.O. Box 87, Concord, MA 01742

To my Mom and Dad for teaching me how to love and appreciate all animals.

Contents

Acknowledgements   11

Foreword by Alexandra Kilgore, D.V.M.   17

Introduction   19

The Formative Years of an Animal Rescuer   21

Little Buster   23

Two Tales of Daisy June   25

Late Night Meanderings   29

My Inner Voice   30

Benny and Pasha   32

How a Cat Named Pud Got Me Started   34

Mother, Turtle in Bathtub!   37

Brandy and Brunswick   39

Stranger   42

Pig Talk   44

Harriet and the Meatloaf   46

Blizzard Rescue 47

Another Daisy and Then Some 50

Sebastian 51

Running Away From Home 53

Coyote Resort 55

The Cat Takes the Lead 58

Murder at Fort Devens 60

My Intuition 63

Catnapping 64

Learning the Hard Way 66

Coming to My Rescue 67

Naked Ladies of P-Town 68

The Cat That Talked, Honest! 73

Rosy 75

Twenty-Three Cats in One Summer 78

Skunk Hotel 81

The Prodigal Snail in the Brandy Snifter 84

The Psychic Pull 86

Rosie, the Little Grey Ghost 87

Munchkin 89

My Hind Leg 92

The Man with Too Many Teeth   93

Good for Me, Good for My Cats   95

The Vegetarian Siamese   98

Floy's Famous Orphanage   100

The Day Geo Died   101

The Great Rabbit Rescue   104

The Christmas Bag Cat   107

Susie   109

Cats Against the Odds   114

My New Home   116

The Last Rescue   119

Adopt-A-Cat   121

Acknowledgements

Perhaps the most valuable gift from this life-long (89-years young) endeavor of mine has been the great long-term friendship I have forged with so many of my volunteers and contributors through our common love of animals. There is no way I can name all of you, but I want you to know how much I deeply appreciate what you have done for me and for our furry friends. I extend a very heartfelt thanks to all of you for your help and friendship.

Many, many, "thank-yous," to Marian Scott without whom this book would never have happened. She pushed me after hearing some of my tales and patiently began putting them into her computer as I dictated. She has been very much a part of this happy endeavor. Thanks also to Kris Cooley for her part in the project.

To my good friend, Puss Pratley, thanks for bringing me together with Ib and Carole Bellew, my publishers. They have made my wish of turning my stories into a book, a reality.

I also have to mention the contribution made by Jim and Vera Coleman one weekend many years ago. They recognized the need for a major overhaul of the cats' living quarters and took it upon themselves to organize and complete the renovation of my garage as a great surprise to me and the cats. I will forever be grateful for the time and energy put into that project and their also ongoing financial support.

To Dr. Kilgore and her staff at the Littleton Animal Hospital for the love and care they have given my animals and the comfort given to me in the sad times. Thank you, Alex.

To Andrea Taylor, who initially baled me out during a hurricane, and stepped in to watch over my furry family — a big thank you for filling the void my absence will create in the animal rescue community by continuing where I have left off.

To Richard A. Campbell, many thanks for all of the trips to the veterinarian, the help in rounding up strays, and learning very quickly what litter pans are for and what to do about them. Also for allowing me to move into my new home with peace the of mind knowing that my cats were going to be well taken care by him.

And finally, one big thank-you to all the animals that have been a part of my life.

Clarence   E. T.

Cooney

Cricket

Gypsy

Makaha

Maurice

Milo

Precious Percy

Raspberry

Sammie

Sammy

Cally

Ellie

Petuli

Piewacket

Princess

Smudge

foreword

To know the soul of a cat is truly special. To have known the souls of many cats, and to have been their savior, is a miracle. Floy Morway is that miracle.

I met Floy in 1983 when I first graduated from Tufts Veterinary School. At that time Floy had eighty cats. She cared for them and placed them as fast as they came in. The task was immense and heartrending. She relied on many volunteers and donations, but carried the majority of the tasks on her own shoulders. As her vet, my hospital provided medical and surgical care for the cats, and we saw her often. She was always upbeat with a joke or a story to tell and always appreciative of whatever we could do. And, most important, she was always ready to rescue another cat. As time went on, and Floy started to have some health problems, she left messages on her answering machine that she could not take any more cats. But that did not stop the many people who would just abandon their cats on her doorstep. In spite of the added burden, Floy never complained and continued placing and finding homes for those needy animals.

I had a lot to learn as a new veterinarian. Working with Floy through the years since then has been an honor. Sharing her love with her loving felines, she has helped me to learn that compassion is the greater part of medicine, and that faced with difficult choices, the dignity and comfort of the animal is most important. I have much to be thankful to Floy for. She has always been there for me as a veterinarian and, even more important, for her feline friends. She really is a Kitty Angel.

Alexandra Kilgore, D.V.M.

Introduction

Even as a young child, I was always a very level-headed individual, not prone to superstition or inordinately curious about the great unknown. However, when I was just 15, a remarkable event happened that changed me forever. I had become very ill and had to undergo an emergency appendectomy. In those days, surgical procedures were still fairly primitive, and the only available anesthetic was ether. Unfortunately for me, an overdose was administered, and I lay unconscious for three days, hovering between the world I knew and one I hadn't even contemplated.

During that time, I remember experiencing the feeling of walking down a long straight tunnel of bright light. As I neared the tunnel's end, two identical white poodles, dogs I had never seen or even heard of before, appeared in front of me, blocking my way. As I tried to go forward, the dogs barred my progress and literally pushed me back from the light. Just at that moment, the light disappeared, and I suddenly became aware of my father and mother standing over me and crying. When they realized I was still alive, they gasped, smiled, and though still crying, their tears were now caused by overwhelming relief.

This was a turning point in my life. Although I had always felt close to animals, this early spiritual experience set the stage for my complete devotion to caring for animals, especially cats. I knew my destiny was to take care of them in any way I could. Little did I realize that I would become a pioneer in the cat rescue movement. Through the years I have witnessed cats in very distressing conditions. I have been appalled by the incredible neglect, cruelty, the sheer numbers of animals without homes, and the amount of work needing to be done. Once you have read all my stories you will understand how finding strength to do something about these deplorable conditions gave me great purpose in life. I came to realize that what was killing me was keeping me alive.

Most of the stories here are about cats, but there are also some "tales" of other animals as well. All animals can connect with us. One hears of "therapy dogs" that save their masters by barking into the phone, or of dogs that pull drowning babies out of swimming pools. There are also numerous stories of dolphins aiding in the rescue of people at sea. These are not isolated instances, but are tangible proof of the inherent bonds linking all living creatures. For this reason, we must become gentle stewards of the animals in our care. We must advocate for speechless creatures and protect them from abuse. It is our duty and a joyous burden that enhances our lives.

To this day I can't see a white poodle without smiling and tearing up a bit.

The Formative Years of an Animal Rescuer

M y love for animals began when I was quite young. One of my earliest memories is of my father coming into my room gently cradling a small bundle wrapped in a towel. Handing a tiny creature to me he said, "Floy, this is a kitten for you to love and care for as you grow up. Remember that all animals are to be treated with kindness and affection, to be given food and warmth, and that you are responsible for your kitten's safety." Never one to mince words, my father was business-like in his approach to giving me a pet, but his soft side showed clearly in the gentleness he exhibited towards that tiny kitten.

From the moment Dad handed me the tiny bundle I soon named "Tabby," she became a first-rate member of our family. She lived with us for many years, becoming more precious to me as she and I grew up together. Tabby even traveled with us each year by train to our summer cottage in Canada. At that time, animals were not permitted to travel by rail, so my grandmother used a cunning piece of deception. Luckily the trip wasn't long, and my clever Nanny would swaddle poor Tabby in a blanket, cuddle her lovingly as if she were a baby, and board the train with the air of an attentive grandmother.

Amazingly, Tabby put up with this, meekly snuggling next to my grandmother's voluminous bosom, soon falling asleep to the soothing sound of her heartbeat. Periodically, the conductor would inquire politely if the baby needed anything, and Nanny would just rock the bundle lovingly and say, "No, thank you." With the Tabby's full cooperation, we repeated this deception for many summers. I think Tabby understood she had a nice life at our house, and she put up with being wrapped in swaddling clothes for a few hours each year in exchange for all the love and care she received on a daily basis.

From then on my family always had many cats, up to eight at one point, plus a dog. My mother took in the many needy strays that wandered into our lives, and, fortunately, my father loved the animals as much as we did.

Little Buster

All teenage girls have a first crush. We all dream of the perfect guy: brown-eyed, a mop of curly hair, and complete devotion to his lady. Little Buster was my four-legged teenage love. He was part Cocker Spaniel and part something wonderful, with large floppy ears and soft, melting brown eyes that looked right through your heart. When he cocked his head to the side and looked at you, there was no refusing him another cookie or treat. Like the perfect boyfriend, he followed me everywhere, bravely protecting his lady. I thought it was because he loved me, but looking back maybe it was the beef flavored cookies.

One day he even followed me to school. To me this was a sign of true devotion, bravely trudging all that way — which was actually only a few blocks. Naturally, when the bell rang, we all ran inside and the doors were closed leaving him outside, and I assumed he would wander back home. But, of course, I underestimated his determination. Stealthily concealing himself in the nearby bushes, he waited for the next person to enter the building. Using his superior canine skills he scooted in and sniffed his way into my classroom. Carefully examining each student, Little Buster found his lady and settled comfortably at my feet. Fortunately, my teacher was happy to have Little Buster in the classroom as long as he was well behaved. He had earned his reward and was allowed to stay — well, at least until flea season arrived.

Two Tales of Daisy June

Dedicated to my wirehaired fox terrier, without whom I probably wouldn't be here today.

1 walked into a "five-and-ten" many years ago. It seemed that back then every small town in Vermont would have one of those catch-all shops. As I was browsing, I noticed on the floor what appeared to be a dirty mop, but then it moved. Upon closer inspection, the "mop" turned out to be an adorable little puppy.

After making a few inquiries in the store, I discovered that no one knew or cared who owned the female pup. I was smitten and had totally forgotten what I'd come for. I called out to her, "Come on, baby." She got up and followed me across the street to the car where my husband was waiting. "How much did that cost?" he asked, but immediately agreed that whatever price, she was worth it. That proved to be the understatement of all time.

We took our new little puppy home and named her Daisy June, after a character made famous by the comedian Red Skelton. She quickly became devoted to me and kept close to me at all times. I found this very comforting, as my mother and father had passed away just a few months earlier, and I was newly pregnant.

At this time, World War II had just begun, and my husband joined the navy. After he shipped out on a submarine, I found myself alone, missing him terribly, with only my little Daisy June for company. Morning sickness took its toll practically every half-hour. Naturally, I was exhausted and slept soundly whenever I could.

As it was, Daisy June had never barked once in the entire six or seven months that we had her, but one night I heard her going from room to room, barking throughout our small one-story house. I tried to wake up without much luck, until Daisy June came back into our bedroom, barking furiously. Finally rousing myself, I was horrified to see two huge hairy arms taking the screen off my window.

I quickly called my neighbor on the phone, whose back door faced my house. The next thing I saw was a rotund little man in pajamas comes running out of his house, carrying a hunting rifle, and yelling, "Stop or I'll shoot!" The intruder took off across the field. My neighbor telephoned the police who came the next morning and told me how lucky I was. They had been looking for this man. He had murdered two women and was being transferred to a maximum security prison when he escaped. They said that if it had not been for the dog awakening me, I probably would have been number three. Needless to say, Daisy June never left my side and never barked again.

A month or so later, I required a brief hospitalization, and it was necessary to find someone to care for Daisy June while I was away. In those days boarding kennels were non-existent. Unfortunately, my nice neighbor who had come to my rescue was traveling at the time, so I reluctantly asked another couple who lived nearby. They agreed, but my instinct warned me it wasn't a good idea, as the husband was a heavy drinker and was known to have a bad temper. I hadn't learned to trust my instincts yet, and with no other option I left Daisy June with them and went into the hospital.

Daisy June had a skin allergy and had to have medication rubbed on her itchy spots several times a day. They assured me that this procedure would not pose a problem. However, it posed the worst problem.

After being released from the hospital, my first priority was to retrieve my Daisy June. Arriving at the couple's house, stoic faces met me at the door. I was horrified as I learned of her fate. They simply couldn't be bothered to give her the medication, call me, or find her somewhere to go. Apparently her persistent thumping and scratching had gotten on the husband's nerves to such a point that in his frustration and anger he just shot her. Perhaps they thought I'd never get out

·of the hospital, or perhaps they actually had a grudge against me, but the brutality shocks me to this day.

The memory of Daisy June and the grief of her loss in such a manner have never left me. She had protected me and saved my life, but I was unable to protect her.

Late Night Meanderings

I found myself for a brief while living in and apartment where no pets were allowed, but that did not stop me. At that time the only four-legged furry friend I had was a black-and-white rabbit. I would walk him late at night outside on his leash to get some exercise. I am sure the gardeners must have wondered why all the tops of the flowers were disappearing. One night, while out on our evening stroll, I ran into a man walking a skunk on a leash. The two of us looked at each other and burst into laughter. Thus began a ritual every night, weather permitting, the two of us meeting in the garden and walking our unusual pets.

My Inner Voice

Before I totally committed myself to animal rescue, I was a young single mother living in Massachusetts. Things had not worked out with my first husband, but I had a beautiful young son, Jack, and he was the joy of my life. I took a job as a nanny, providing childcare in a small trailer in Wayland. We had two dogs and a cat. It wasn't too long before another man came into my life, and we soon decided to marry. We made plans to move into Boston where work would be easier to find. As much as I would have preferred to remain in the suburbs, my hay fever was so bad that my doctor felt that the move would be beneficial.

As we were packing to leave, my beloved cat Butterscotch decided to disappear. Maybe he thought we were leaving him behind, or perhaps the disruption in our daily routine just frightened him. As soon as we discovered he was missing, we mounted a search and began looking everywhere, but to no avail. Sadly we departed for our new home. After the move, my thoughts continually went back to him, wondering if he was all right and if someone was feeding him. I called my former neighbors, asking them to look out for him and to please let me know of any sightings.

On my fourth day in the city, I felt I needed to go back once more to try to find my old friend. I begged to be driven to Wayland. When we arrived we found all was quiet at my old trailer. After several hours of searching and calling for my cat, my husband-to-be gently urged me that it was time to go back home. Something told me to stay. Not wanting to ignore these feelings, I insisted on being left alone to remain at the trailer until late afternoon. I sat down on the front steps to wait patiently, certain that if my cat were nearby he would come to me.

After a short time, I felt impelled to walk to a small stand of trees and call for Butterscotch. To my joyful surprise, within several minutes of my calling, my furry friend bounded out, none the worse for wear. I scooped him up in my arms, took him into the trailer for some water, and waited for our ride home. From then on he became quite content to be an indoor cat. My intuition had been spot-on, and my inner voice had led me to do what my cat needed. I was learning to trust my instincts.

Benny and Pasha

My son, Jack, also loved animals and frequently brought home stray dogs, knowing I would either adopt them or find them a good home. One day, although I already had four dogs and many cats, Jack brought home a handsome, 6-month-old German Shepherd, whom we named Pasha. At the time, I was living in the suburbs some thirty miles from Cambridge, Massachusetts.

A half mile from my house was a dilapidated old house with a glassed-in front porch. It was owned by an elderly man I knew only as Benny. He had two beautiful German Shepherds, and although his house looked messy, his dogs appeared to be well cared for. So I thought maybe he would provide just the right home for the pup.

Arriving at his house I found Benny on his way out. Responding to my question as to whether he would like another dog, Benny muttered gruffly, "Sure, leave the dog on the porch, I will be right back."

Back home, and thinking about the situation at length, I was certain I had made a big mistake. Benny's house wasn't the right place for Pasha. Therefore, I climbed back into my car and headed back to Benny's house to retrieve him. I found Pasha, tied to the front doorknob on a short leash, unable to sit or lie down, and with no water or food in sight. I knew immediately that I needed to take him away. However, when I realized the door to the glassed-in porch was locked, I had to come up with another plan.

I went home and called the police. They advised, "Get your dog and don't have anything more to do with that man." I panicked, but not for long since it was getting, dark and I knew I had to hurry. I called a friend, Jean, for help. Armed with a flashlight, gloves, and a hammer, Jean and I nervously drove to Benny's house. Upon arriving, I handed Jean the flashlight to hold, then used the hammer to smash one of the porch's windowpanes.

Suddenly, the flashlight began to dance. Jean whispered, "He's coming, he's coming!" Benny was one angry man, shouting, "What's going on? What are you doing?" By this time I had Pasha untied and was heading out the door. I shouted back to Benny, "Stay away from the dog! I just found out he has a disease that's transferable to human beings. I have to get him to the vet immediately!"

This ruse quieted Benny for a few seconds — long enough for us to hop into the car to make our getaway. As we drove off, we could hear Benny shouting even louder, "He *messed* in my shoe!" — except with more explicit language.

How a Cat Named Pud Got Me Started

Ibelieve that animal people must have a specific trait for rescue work, which they somehow pass on to their offspring. Jack was exposed to all kinds of animal rescues as a young child, so it came as no surprise to me when he wandered in one day with a small kitten. The little fellow, whom we named Pud, was 6-weeks old and solid black. He had huge triple paws; which means he had extra toes on each foot. From the size of those feet, we knew he would grow into a large fellow. As a kitten his one trick was to sit on a stool and swat at us with his enormous paws, merrily spewing spit as we tried to avoid his blows.

This was the 60s, and I had just moved to a small development in Littleton, Massachusetts. As well as Pud, I also had a 12-week-old rather large and drooly Saint Bernard puppy, Brandy, and a cocker spaniel mix called, Brunswick. The three animals eventually made peace and became best friends. We would often find Pud snuggled down in Brandy's soft underbelly.

Pud soon outgrew the spitting and swatting behavior, as well as the stool, and became a very handsome and elegant companion. A couple of my friends fell in love with his dashing good looks and dignified personality. They begged me to let them know if, on the unlikely chance I came across another Pud look-a-like, to please tell them. I never expected to find an exact duplicate of my Pud, but I filed the information away for the future. These people would make some kitty very happy.

One dark, rainy evening, I heard Pud calling from the back door to be let in for the night. To my surprise, he had brought home a friend — another solid black kitten. I had settled the new kitty down when the next afternoon we had a repeat performance, possibly from the same litter! Sadly it is not uncommon for people to drop off unwanted animals in rural neighborhoods mistakenly assuming they can "fend for themselves."

After several days with my new charges, I realized that it was time to call my friends and tell them about Pud's kitten buddies. I bought some doughnuts, made a fresh pot of coffee, and invited them over to see the kitties. They loved them, and as they were leaving with their new charges, they paused and asked me if I could help one of their elderly neighbors. The poor women had to move and had two cats that were very dear to her, but, alas, her landlord didn't allow cats in her new apartment. I hesitated only for a moment, and then happily agreed. I thought to myself, "That should be easy." Within days I had placed the two newcomers in loving homes. Friends told friends; friends told strangers; and stranger told other strangers. Like gossip in a small community, word got around how I was taking in strays and finding homes for them. I was off and running as the "Cat Lady."

Mother,
Turtle in Bathtub!

My usual habit when I arrived home was to head straight for the bathroom. One day I found the door closed and a piece of paper taped to it with the notice, Mother, Turtle in bathtub! There were no other details, but knowing Jack, he just assumed I would be able to handle the situation and do the best thing for my new aquatic friend. I opened the door, and, sure enough, there in the bathtub sat a very large snapping turtle. I smiled to myself and said, "Oh, well, what now?"

I called a friend to consult on solutions, and we decided the best thing to do was to take him for another ride. I found an old cardboard container, like the ones that hold soda cans, and placed the turtle in it. My car was quite small, but I managed to put the box on the floor behind the driver's seat. I then headed out to the country, hopefully to find a pond where I could leave my newly acquired housemate. As I drove around, I wasn't having much luck, for I didn't know the area, and I thought if I pulled over and flagged someone driving by,

I might be able to get some assistance. Sure enough, after waiting just a short while, a young mother and her 14-year-old son came to my rescue. I explained my dilemma, and by this time the turtle had crawled out of the box and was well-wedged under the driver's seat, so I definitely needed help to extricate him. They said that they knew just the spot to take him, and the young lad agreed to ride with me in my car carrying the turtle on his lap.

The first pond that we came to looked fine, but when we got out of the car to introduce him to his new surroundings, a man told us that we couldn't leave him there, because he would kill all the baby ducklings in the pond; so we drove off. Luckily the women also knew of another pond nearby that was more secluded, and we were able to accomplish our rescue mission.

Later that day, as I was going over the experience in my mind, it came to me how lucky we were that this large hard shelled creature seemed to realize our intentions and desire to help him. Never once did he act like a snapping turtle might, and stayed very docile with the boy and me.

Brandy and Brunswick

Brandy, my Saint Bernard, was a thoroughly lovable pet. He had a sidekick, a cocker spaniel mix named Brunswick, whom I'd acquired as a puppy at an arcade on Salisbury Beach on the northeastern coast of Massachusetts. Brunswick had been a prize offering for tourists able to knock balls off in a particular arcade game. I asked the arcade owner how much he'd sell the puppy for. The man replied, "He's not for sale." I announced that the dog was going home with me, one way or the other. The arcade owner said, "Lady, if you have $25, he's yours." I had exactly $25 with me, and though I had designated the money for meals, snacks, and a day at the beach, I gave it to the man anyway, picked up the pup, and went home with a happy heart.

Brunswick was adorable. Brandy took to him immediately, and the two became inseparable. They loved to ride in my car so much that I took to leaving the car door open when the car was in the closed garage, which had always been their sleeping quarters. The car's back seat soon became their permanent bed.

At the time, I was still living in Littleton, Massachusetts, about four houses in from a busy main road. Living on that road was a family with a little Scottish terrier, who had never been spayed. Whenever she came into season, Brandy would want to visit her. Accordingly, whenever I knew it was about that time, I would tie Brandy up or walk him on a leash. One morning, I told Brandy it would be his last day of running around for a while, and to make the most of it. So off went Brandy and Brunswick, in high glee, I thought to the backwoods. Suddenly, Brunswick appeared at the door. I asked him where Brandy was. Brunswick just stood there, looking at me. Brandy wasn't in sight and I sensed something was wrong.

I immediately telephoned a neighbor who lived along the main road. She went out to look for Brandy and quickly returned to the phone, reporting that he was lying by the side of the road. I ran out, only to find that it was too late to save him, Brandy was already dead. Good neighbors helped to carry him home. I called Jack, who at the time was attending college and living in Cambridge, Massachusetts. He immediately came right out and spent most of the afternoon digging a grave and then burying our Brandy.

Jack stayed with me that night. At about 6 a.m., we were awakened by the distinct howl of a Saint Bernard. We both opened our bedroom doors and met in the hallway. Jack said,

"Mother, I buried him," but we both knew we had heard the familiar sound. Suddenly, we heard it again. Following the sound, we discovered it was coming from the back seat of the car in the garage, where Brandy and Brunswick always slept together. But now the sound was coming from Brunswick, howling just as Brandy had! Brunswick's howling continued for three days and then suddenly stopped; Brunswick was back to his own voice.

This was my first inkling that animals have their own way of saying goodbye. And in a strange way, Brunswick's howling helped ease the pain of our loss.

Stranger

While my son, Jack, was a student at Boston University, he lived in a house with several other students. The housemates had five cats, creatures that seemed to have arrived for a handout, but never left. Each morning the students set out five dishes of food. And then one day, they counted noses and discovered a sixth cat. Setting down a sixth dish, the students named the new arrival, Stranger. Later, when Jack moved across town, they decided that Stranger should stay with the group because Jack's job would keep him away from home a lot, and no one else would be there to keep him company. It was clear, however, that Stranger had become very attached to Jack.

Within three weeks of Jack's move, his former housemates told him that Stranger had vanished the day following Jack's departure. From what followed, I maintain to this day, never underestimate what an animal can do when it feels a true bond.

Settled in his new place, one evening Jack heard a loud meow. He went to the door and opened it to discover a happy, purring, yet very thin and hungry Stranger. The cat, of course, had never been to his house, but still found his way across Cambridge, from Inman Square to Porter Square, to locate the one person who ever truly cared for him in his entire cat-life! And, of course, he stayed there with Jack. Home is where the "heart" is.

Pig Talk

The first day of an extended visit to a friend's family farm, I was stopped in my tracks by a big handsome pig. Our eyes met, and I felt instantly drawn. I left my friend in the dust in my haste to get closer to him. The family all laughed at me, but allowed me to go into the pen. I patted him tenderly for several minutes, to which he returned thankful snorts. The next morning at feeding time I saw him watching out through the fence, looking at me. I became the designated daily pig feeder for my stay there, during which time we developed a fond affection for each other with ritual eye contact, touch, soft words, pats, grunts, and snorts. I was so charmed with him. Realizing his fate, I tried to figure out a way to take him home with me. Alas, none was found and the time came for me to go back to my house. Leaving him was a sad day. I was told that for a full week after I left he went regularly to our meeting spot to look for me. Pigs have feelings, too!

Harriet and
the Meatloaf

H arriet was a fifteen-pound cat who loved food, any kind of food. One day after I'd made a meatloaf, a neighbor called, inviting me for coffee. "Yes, please," I replied enthusiastically. So, I quickly propped the oven door open, to let the meatloaf cool while I went next door for a visit. My oven was a small wall model, mounted up and off to the side of the counter.

We had a lovely time sharing stories, and naturally I lost track of time. I remembered that I had a couple coming over to look at cats, hopefully choosing one to adopt. I hurried home, and as I came through the door, out of the corner of my eye I caught a movement coming from the wall near the counter. There was Harriet, ensconced in the oven, chomping her way through my meatloaf.

Thank God she had the sense to wait until the meatloaf cooled before jumping up into the oven, for she was completely unscathed, except for her tomato stained face. Indeed, she seemed ecstatic munching away to her heart's content. It goes without saying that she didn't ask for food for the rest of the day.

Blizzard Rescue

One day, in the midst of New England's famous blizzard of 1978, a friend called from New Hampshire to let me know about a cocker spaniel that had been in its doghouse throughout the storm. A friend offered to drive me to New Hampshire to save the dog. As we reached the house, we saw one car in the driveway and tracks indicating that another car had recently pulled out. Apparently, the residents had been able to dig out enough to venture elsewhere, with no thought to the dog's safety.

Approaching the backyard, my friend and I beheld the frightened eyes of the cocker spaniel, peering at us from within the doghouse. We saw no tracks leading to or from the doghouse. Realizing the spaniel's distress, I didn't spend another minute worrying about the dog's owners, and I didn't care if we were arrested for rescuing the poor creature.

Immediately, I plowed my way through with snow up to my hips, only to find that the doghouse contained no blanket, no food dish, and no water. Holding out my arms the spaniel bounded into them. I unsnapped the chain, then we made our way back through the snow and climbed into my friend's car. She had the motor running for a quick getaway, certain that the police would be hot on our trail.

I'd brought food and water with me, and the cocker spaniel devoured the food and lapped up the water. Back in Massachusetts, I took him directly to my vet, who reported that the dog was fine, except for being severely dehydrated and extremely hungry. I next called a friend on Cape Cod and told her I had a present for her. She drove to my home right away, fell in love with the cocker spaniel, and adopted him on the spot.

My friend in New Hampshire later notified me that three days had passed before the people even began inquiring if anyone had seen their dog. As for me, I feel strongly that certain people should never own a pet.

Framed on my side table there still is an enlarged snapshot of the now healthy and happy cocker spaniel, sent to me years ago by his loving new owner.

To my friend and saviour, with love and gratitude
Floy
Sukey

Another Daisy and Then Some

No one wanted to get near her. With panic and fear in her eyes, the large dog crouched on the lawn at the library. Everyone stayed away, thinking she was dangerous. Fortunately, someone thought to call me. I went right up to the dog, spoke to her gently, and gave her a piece of chicken. I said, "Come on, baby," words of encouragement that got her into my car.

Once home, I settled her down for the night in my dining room, intending to take her to the vet in the morning. But in the middle of the night, I was awakened by small cries and arose to discover an exhausted mother pooch and eight squirming pups. I put out an SOS for old newspapers, which were needed to top the plastic covering on my new dining room floor. To contain the puppies, a child's large circular collapsible playpen came in handy.

After eight weeks, I had placed all the pups in pairs, with four happy families. The mother dog herself turned out to be a wonderful gentle pet, which my granddaughter fell in love with. She named her Daisy, and had her for many years.

Sebastian

A woman knowing my involvement with animals called to say that she had just returned from a place in New Hampshire where a man had five, 9-month-old, Newfoundland puppies. The puppies had outgrown their cages to the point that they could not stand upright. I immediately telephoned everyone I knew who might be interested in rescuing Newfoundland puppies. The five of us gathered, each taking a separate car, and drove to New Hampshire to look at the dogs. By day's end, all but one of the puppies had been adopted.

The pup that was left sat at the back of the cage, looking at me. Since just shortly beforehand I'd lost my Saint Bernard, I wasn't really ready for another dog. I went over to the cage and put my hand in, to say a goodbye for now, until I could find another adoptive family. But, when the pup picked up his paw and placed it on my arm, that was that. He'd found his new adoptive home.

This little guy, whom I named Sebastian, had hip dysplasia

and ran in a peculiar fashion. This is a common problem in large breed dogs, but being kept in too-small-a cage, unfortunately, had affected all the puppies. He also had heartworm so severe that the vet said he wouldn't live long enough to receive the full treatment. He didn't seem to be suffering, though, and he played happily and ate well. Despite my initial fears, and to my great delight, Sebastian not only lived through the treatment, he thrived as my beloved pet for nine years.

Running Away from Home

A beautiful long-haired calico, Cynthia, was one of my favorites. It was Cynthia who taught me that animals are much more knowledgeable and sensitive than we humans give them credit for. My neighbors had a male cat named Stanley that, since kittenhood, had demonstrated extreme behavioral problems, including viciousness. Inasmuch as his owners didn't take good care of him, the cat would often visit my house to be fed.

One day, as I was holding Cynthia in my arms, Stanley arrived at my door. I put Cynthia down and prepared to get the cat his little dish of food. All of a sudden, Cynthia went over to Stanley and whacked him showing her disapproval. Though I scolded Cynthia, she merely looked at me and walked out the door. I knew by her demeanor that she was angry and had no intention of returning. Almost immediately, I dropped everything and went looking for her. Over the next few days I posted signs and photos everywhere. Someone said they thought they'd seen her at the Nashoba

Valley ski area. The terrain was rough, and I wandered all over the hill, as far as I could go, trying to find my Cynthia. I hunted all over Littleton for three weeks. I did not give up, but I was brokenhearted.

Just after feeding my cats one morning, the telephone rang; a woman from the other side of town told me she had found a cat matching Cynthia's description. I immediately drove to her house, and there was my poor Cynthia, all skin and bones. With great relief I scooped her up and took her home, setting her down gently, among her old friends.

At first, Cynthia would have nothing to do with anyone or anything. After three days, however, she suddenly remembered who I was. Although she slowly came back to life, she had clearly suffered greatly from the ordeal. It took many weeks, and while she physically remained much more subdued than in earlier days, she was happy and content and never ran away again. I apologized for scolding her and vowed I'd never scold a cat again.

Coyote Resort

My house in Concord, Massachusetts, had two acres of wetlands behind it, which were inhabited by all sorts of wild creatures, big and small. Looking from my kitchen window, one could view deer, rabbits, raccoons, chipmunks, all sorts of birds, and even an occasional wild turkey. Sometimes a neighbor's dog would wander by, searching for the treats I left at the back door for the raccoons. At the back of the property, about forty feet from the house, sat a large old red doghouse. I always kept old blankets it, thinking that little creatures could find shelter there in the cold, or give birth in its warmth and safety.

One afternoon, a friend came by to help clean the cats' cages in the "cattery." As she was washing up afterwards in the kitchen sink, above which was a window overlooking my back yard, she exclaimed, "Floy, there's a coyote in the doghouse!" Looking out the kitchen window, I saw a very old male coyote walk out of the doghouse, head to the tiny brook at the side of my property for a drink, and then turn and walk back into the doghouse. He looked exhausted.

My friend went to leave by the kitchen door, but when she opened it, I saw the coyote wake up and sniff at the air. Getting stiffly to his feet, he walked a few paces toward the side of the house. She froze at my command and backed slowly into the house, closing the door softly. We both went over to the kitchen window to watch what the coyote would do next. He seemed bored and tired. Turning around, he retreated into the doghouse and flopped down. Moving quickly, my friend exited the side door again, went to her car and got in. This time the coyote didn't move.

The next day I was in my basement tending to my feline housemates and enjoying a peanut butter-and-jelly sandwich. The coyote was back in the doghouse, so I decided to see if he was hungry enough to enjoy a taste of my sandwich. He was and he did. Over the course of the next few days I fed him more sandwiches, cat food, and dog food. Strangely, I felt no fear, and I sensed that he would be grateful for the food.

What amazed me as I looked back over the situation was the fact that I disobeyed all rules and walked out to the doghouse to feed this wild animal that supposedly attacked humans. I am known for breaking laws, and I just knew he wasn't going to hurt me. I took the gamble, and it paid off.

A few weeks later, a young female coyote came and slept in the doghouse. However, I never saw the old male again, and I think he may have spent his last days at my "coyote resort." It gratifies me to think that I provided "assisted living" to him at the end of his life.

The Cat Takes the Lead

As my reputation as the Cat Lady of Concord grew, I began receiving telephone calls asking for my help from far and wide. Once I received a call from the owner of a local shop located in a small strip mall in nearby Acton, Massachusetts. He explained that he had seen a stray cat hanging around, looking in the dumpsters for food. I agreed to help and gathered up my gloves, cat carrier, and a trusty can of smelly cat food (the smellier the better — when you set a humane trap with sardines it guarantees success!) Getting in my car, I sped up Route 2 toward Acton to retrieve the cat.

Arriving at the shop, it took me only a matter of moments to locate my quarry. The poor little girl was a thin orange-and-white-tabby with a slightly flabby belly — a sign she might have just given birth. She wound herself around my ankles and seemed friendly, so I knelt down and felt her stomach to make certain my supposition was correct. She was indeed a nursing mother, and her babies had to be hidden somewhere nearby. I knew I had to find them.

Mother cats will carefully conceal their new babies to protect them from predators. Therefore, the only way I would find the babies was for the mother cat to lead me to them. I had a sudden brainstorm and raced to my car to get my tiny dog's harness and lead. Gingerly, I slipped the harness over the tiny cat and took a deep breath, praying she would lead me to her babies. As if understanding perfectly, she began walking toward the back of the building, leading me to an open bulkhead door and there she stopped. I peered down into the basement and there, snuggled in an old box was her newly born litter of kittens, sleeping peacefully. I breathed a sigh of relief and gathered up the warm little bundles, cradling the five of them in my arms, as I walked with their mother toward my car.

Murder at Fort Devens

I was living near Fort Devens in Ayer, Massachusetts, when one horribly rainy day, the Ayer Chief of Police called me. "A murder has occurred at Fort Devens," he said, "and a mother cat with kittens have been left alone. Can you come and get them?" Sighing deeply, I replied, "I'm full," but then added, "If you cared enough to call me, I will be there." I next called a friend who had a station wagon, and together we went to the scene of the crime.

Upon entering the tiny house, we saw blood everywhere. The room that should have been the dining room held a pool table. In one bedroom, containing bunk beds where two little boys had slept, we noticed there were no bed linens, just the blue ticking mattress and pillows. In the other room, some twenty wig-heads occupied every open surface. I asked the chief how she had died. He told me she was hit over the head with the television set. A giant size-box of Tide had been spilled all over the kitchen floor, and dirty dishes were piled high. The scene was chaotic, but the mother cat and her kittens were obviously used to it. They seem unperturbed, walking around, cleaning themselves and checking us out.

Then came the shocker; in the backyard, in the pouring rain, huddled two large vicious-looking German Shepherds tied by heavy short chains to a pole. "Don't go near them, they're dangerous!" the chief cautioned. But I sensed neediness in them, almost as though they were waiting for me, and I proceeded to walk right over to them. The "dangerous" dogs licked my hand. With the rain drenching all of us, I said, "I'm taking them with me, too." The police chief responded, "No one will believe me when I tell them this."

Without the police chief's help, my friend and I took the dogs directly to the station wagon, along with the mother cat and 6-week-old kittens. The little family nestled cozily in a box. We drove directly to the home of a friend whose German Shepherd had recently died. The dog had been a watchdog for his business, a gravel pit. I said, "I have brought you two presents. They are hungry and wet but eager to be loved. You are going to love them." He did and the pair turned out to be great dogs.

The next day, the Ayer Police Chief called again. His officers had found another cat, presumably the father, in the basement. As it turned out all were full-bred Persians, the father was all black and the mother was white. I traveled back out to Fort Devens to get the dad, and he became one of my favorite cats. I called him, Special, and he certainly deserved the name. As for the mother and her kittens, I did not have any trouble placing them in good homes.

My Intuition

One day some people came to me to adopt a pair of cats. I had a feeling about them, but they promised they would provide a good home, and they gave me $50 toward my shelter expenses. I ignored my apprehensions and let them take the cats. Six months later I got a call from somebody to come pick up two cats that had been abandoned after the owners just upped and moved out. I called my trusty volunteer Linda, and we headed out to pick up the cats. Well, low and behold, they were those same two cats that had been adopted. I should really learn to trust my intuition.

Catnapping!

Neighbors complained of the smell and constant crying of a cat living with a man known to be verbally abusive and an alcoholic. Though I wanted to meet with the man to discuss the cat's welfare, given the circumstances, I was certain he would never invite me into his house. Yet hearing of several such complaints, I decided it was time to relieve this man of his cat. But how?

I began by snooping around enough to ascertain that the man usually sat in a chair in the front room. In the kitchen at the back of the house, was a large window that was often left wide open — an invitation for me to strike while the weather was warm!

I enlisted the help of my friend, Gigi, a smooth talker. While Gigi went to the front door on the pretense of asking directions from the cat's owner, I entered the house through the kitchen window and quickly found the enormous orange tomcat. As I tucked him under my arm and scrambled back out of the window, the cat didn't protest in the least. The entire rescue operation took less than five minutes.

The next day, I brought the cat to my vet, who found him unaltered and malnourished, but otherwise, a big loveable slob. The cat, by now dubbed Morris, lived with me for quite a while until I found him a happy new home. Luckily, no repercussion ensued from the original owner, even though our rescue mission could have really been viewed as "catnapping."

Learning the Hard Way

One way of finding exposure for my cats and kittens that needed new homes was to take them to cat shows. I was not entering them in the shows, but just taking advantage of the larger audiences of "Cat Lovers." They would sit in their cages adorably irresistible, and I would wait for some kind soul to be unable to fight the urge to take one of them home. Unfortunately, on this occasion I made the mistake of feeding them before we set off on the trip. They were not happy travelers, and both cats vomited in their cages and all over my car. Linda and I pulled over to the side of the road since there was no question of continuing at that point. It took us half the afternoon to clean up the mess and make the cats presentable again. Needless to say, by the time we arrived it was much too late. The cats came home with us, and you can be sure that we both agreed, never to make that mistake again.

Coming to
My Rescue

I was invited to go to Framingham to give a "cat talk" at the library and answer questions. I was the last one to leave the building around 11 p.m. It was a small branch library in an isolated part of town. I got to my car only to find out to my horror that I had locked my keys inside. The houses around were all dark and quiet, for most people were in for the night, but I did hear laughter and noise coming from a beer joint next to the library. Deciding that I had no choice, I headed over to there, walked passed all the motorcycles parked outside, up to the front door, flung it open, and just stood in the doorway, waiting.

Gradually the noise level of the patrons came to a low hum giving me a chance to speak. I said "I am pretty sure that someone in here knows how to break into a locked car." Five takers jumped up, rushed to the door, and escorted me out to my car. In no time I was seated behind the wheel, slowly pulling out of the lot, waving goodbye and thank you. I drove on home with a smile on my face, wondering did those men all love cats — or perhaps it was my blond hair, black dress, and youthful looks?

Naked Ladies
of P-Town

One summer, my son and daughter-in-law decided to rent a house for a weekend in Provincetown, and they asked me to accompany them. At the time, my granddaughter, Tacita, was only a toddler, and I think they offered the trip to me in part because they wanted my expert babysitting services so they could enjoy a bit of free time alone together. I was only too happy to agree.

Arriving early on a Saturday morning at the small cottage, I climbed out of the car's back seat and looked around the side yard. I saw a yellow cat that obviously had sustained a mouth injury crouched beneath a partially collapsed woodpile. I talked to the cat, and though he cried, he didn't come to me. I went into the house, put water in a bowl, opened a can of tuna fish we had brought for picnic sandwiches, and took them out to the poor pitiful thing. I always have a supply of dry cat food with me, but I knew that with the injured mouth he would be unable to chew.

Starving, the brave little fellow attempted to eat, but could only lick a tiny bit of water and some juice from the tuna. His jaw was swollen and angry-looking, and I knew it was infected. Going back to the car, I took a cat carrier out of the trunk and brought it outside. I then lured him into it and shut the door, keeping him safe until I could find the owner or get him to a vet. I walked out the front door and set off to ask the neighbors who owned this cat.

I knocked on the front door of the house next door, but with no luck. I continued on. At the second cottage, I saw cat figurines displayed on the windowsills and thought this could be the cat's home. I knocked on the door, received no answer, but noticed that the door was open. I called out, "Hello." From the back of the house came a woman answering, "Hello to you." And, to my amazement, a very well endowed, rather short, pudgy middle aged woman appeared, stark naked. Looking her square in the eyes, I said, "I found an injured cat, and I'm wondering whether you might be the cat's owner or that you might be able to help me get in touch with a local veterinarian. She replied, "No, we are not the owners, but my mother might be able to help you find a vet. Follow me."

I followed her to the back of the house, noting that the back view was much like the front view. It was all I could do to restrain myself from giggling at the absurdity of the situation. Little did I know that the situation was to become even more absurd, for as her mother arose from her lounge chair in the backyard to greet me, I realized that the even older lady was naked. While I was talking to the two of them, a young man descended the outdoor stairs of the house next door. The gentleman, fully dressed in a business suit, waved, said "Hello," and just kept going as if there was nothing out of the ordinary.

Putting on my best "poker face," I asked the mother about the cat, and although she also had no idea who owned him, she was extraordinarily sympathetic and offered to help in any way she could. She did have a number for a veterinarian, which we called to no avail. After chatting with my new found "bosom buddies" a few minutes longer, I let myself out the back gate and headed for the next house.

After a few more attempts, I became frustrated. If no one was answering their front doors, it was probably because they were all at the beach. It was becoming obvious to me that I would have to take the cat to a vet myself. When I got back to the house, I tried the vet's number again, and this time I got an answer, and they were open on Saturdays. I asked Jack to drive us to the vet. It was only a short distance away, and when we arrived, the vet was most anxious to help the poor little fellow. He told us to call him on Monday morning to check on the little guy's progress, and we felt that the cat was now in safe hands.

That night, I had trouble sleeping because I realized that I would have to adopt the cat if I were unable to find his true owner. I already had about forty cats at the shelter, and even though I could always make room for one more, I felt I owed the owners another try to find them. The next morning I set off again on my quest, but by the afternoon, I returned to the house in a depressed mood because I still hadn't found any clues.

On Monday morning I called the veterinarian and was happy to have the good news that the cat was doing very well. He also asked me if I had found the owner, since someone had telephoned him, offering to adopt the cat. I was stunned by this information, as no one that I had interviewed had seemed to know or want the cat. I told the vet I would have my son drive me there to pick up the cat and pay him for his services. The kind-hearted vet refused to accept any money, saying that I had already paid in full rescuing the cat and trying to find his owner, but I could come by to pick up the cat.

Upon arriving at the vet's, Jack and I noticed another car parked in the driveway. We went inside to the waiting room and sat down. The door to the room opened, and in came the vet, followed by two large women in brightly colored caftans. One was carrying a fancy cat carrier and the other, a sparkly blue collar. It took me just a moment to realize they were the naked ladies in clothes! They explained to me that their cat had died of old age a few months earlier and that they missed him greatly. Would it be all right with me if they adopted the injured cat? The vet attested to their excellent care of their previous pet, and truthfully, I was grateful to not have another mouth to feed. However, I did ask for "visiting rights," which were graciously granted. During many subsequent summer trips to Provincetown, I often visited the cat, now known as "Benny."

The Cat That Talked, Honest!

I once had a Siamese cat named Suki, who appeared to be able to talk. She often made voice-like sounds when she wanted something, food, or affection, or when she didn't get her way. She showed great promise — the smartest cat I ever knew.

She had a rabbit's foot key chain, her favorite toy. I kept it in a drawer. When she wanted it she would sit up on the counter by the drawer and make a little asking sound. When I heard that sound, I knew she wanted her rabbit's foot, and I'd open the drawer. She would then go into the drawer and find it — even after I had buried it. Her routine involved carrying it around the house, tossing it up in the air, and rolling around, all the usual playing activities. When she was done, she didn't leave it as other animals usually did, but carried it right back to its drawer, which I left open, and placed it in so that it would be safe for the next time.

Having heard that Siamese cats can be taught to talk, I figured Suki would be a likely candidate if ever there was one. I decided the time was right to try. I began very slowly, "I love you." She looked at me quizzically. I repeated, "I love you."

I repeated and repeated. This went on for several days. I even had a friend, Judy, join me in the effort. Suki actually was beginning to get the idea, we thought, so we tried all the more. Her purring changed and was combined with a funny new whine. She was definitely experimenting.

However, after a while the process became more of a habit than an expectation. One hot day in July when the doors and windows were wide open, and I was giving Suki her usual lessons, the phone rang. It was my neighbor. She said "Floy, I've been listening to you say 'I love you' for the past few weeks. Who are you talking to?" All I could do was laugh.

We finally just gave up, but as habit would have it, the words slipped out every now and then. One of these times when Suki responded, Judy and I decided that with a little imagination Suki's utterings did indeed sound like "I love you." Honest! As for my neighbor, her inquisitive call was the beginning of a lasting friendship, and for quite a while after that summer we would get together for coffee and have a good chuckle over exactly who it was that I loved!

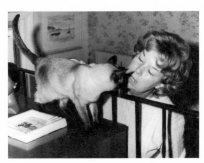

Rosy

A small black cat, Rosy, was brought to me by some people who claimed that she was vicious and bit them all the time. It took me just one day to decide that there was nothing vicious about Rosy; she was as gentle and sweet as could be. For some reason, these people just wanted to get rid of her. When a cat like that comes into my life, I tend to bond more closely with it. Rosy was a very curious kitty. She once followed me down to the laundry, as she pretty much followed me everywhere. After turning on the water, I bent down for an instant to pick up another item to put in — which I did and then closed the cover. But the cover wouldn't close entirely, there was a little black paw in the way. I quickly flipped it open to discover that she was fine except for being a little wet. It was a lesson well-learned for me. Through this and many other similar experiences, Rosy became very special to me. Sadly, I only had her for about a year due to a very unfortunate event.

I had been feeding an older male stray for a couple of years and decided I should try to get him neutered because we didn't need more kittens without homes. I lured him into a Havahart trap, brought him into my house and let him go — big mistake. He simply did not want to be confined. He had been on his own long enough, and when he found himself confined indoors he said, "No, no, no I've got to get out of here." He was so desperate that he managed to squirm through a tiny opening in the wall which was covered with heavy wire mesh that he pushed aside. I knew there was a reason to get that plastering project done.

He then crawled down the space between the walls, allowing his escape. To my chagrin, Rosy had seen him go, and, either because of her natural curiosity or because she had fallen in love, she decided to follow him. She had never been outside before and had none of the smarts of Mr. No-No. It must have been very scary for her. It took me three days before I realized that she was gone, for there was always food out for her, and I assumed she was following her usual routine of sleeping next to the heat vents and eating as she needed.

When I realized that she was gone, I panicked. I called and called and looked and looked. I searched everywhere high and low, inside and out. I had every volunteer looking and calling for her as well. One morning about a week later, I suddenly awoke out of a deep sleep and sat straight up in bed. I had seen, right in front of me, Rosy, little Rosy looking straight at me with baleful eyes. She said to me, "Mommy, Mommy, help me." Then she faded away. I burst into tears.

I continued my search and even hired a psychic to help me find her, but we had no luck. This is one kitty that will always live in my heart. It is proof to me again that animals have souls, and we can and do connect with one another.

Twenty-Three Cats
in One Summer

Coming home late one evening, I found a box with a cat in it on my doorstep. I thought, good people know where I am, and I proceeded happily to take the cat inside. The next night, the phone rang at 9 p.m. A little girl's voice announced that there was a box in my backyard holding a mother cat and her litter of kittens. When I went outside to check, sure enough, there they were, and I greeted them warmly.

For the next two months, sometimes as often as three times a week, my phone rang at 9 p.m. Always the same little girl's voice, she announced that one or more cats had been left in a box somewhere in my backyard. This scenario continued until a total of twenty-three cats.

One of the last 9 p.m. calls had informed me that another box with a mother cat and kittens had been left in the farmland next door to my house. By this time, all the summer rescues had left me physically and emotionally exhausted. As I went to retrieve the box, I discovered, to my dismay, that

I didn't have the strength to carry box, mother, and kittens back to my house.

I went to my neighbor, tearful and frustrated. He kindly carried the box to my house for me. And then he said, "Floy, come home with me. You are going to sit for a bit and have a glass of wine and relax." I did so gladly, knowing all the cats were safe. As I sat there sipping my wine in tears, I poured out the story of the little girl's nightly telephone calls. My friend was truly shocked. I moaned how in the world could I stop this? It was getting beyond me, way more than any single person could reasonably manage.

Shortly after this episode, the cat deliveries stopped. That probably had something to do with the fact that, at the end of our last phone conversation, I had mentioned to the little girl that the police knew who she was and that, were I to find any more cats in my yard, she'd have to answer to them.

I later told the story to a friend of mine at the MSPCA about my plight, and she put two and two together remembering she had seen a woman and a little girl standing outside their entrance. The pair were approaching people and telling them that they knew someone who could provide a perfect home for their cats. A shelter worker said the woman and her daughter had been there for almost two months doing this. Evidently, the woman knew the MSPCA only kept animals a week before euthanizing them, and with a good heart, she felt she was saving their lives. I could never fault her for her kindness, and she would be happy to know that every one of those twenty-three cats and kittens went to a wonderful home. She had saved all of their lives, but almost killed me in the process!

Skunk Hotel

My shelter was in the basement of my home with a large chain-link outdoor pen attached to the back of the house. The basement door was left open in the daytime for the cats to go in and out as they pleased. One day I was in the cattery feeding the guests while talking on the phone as I had a habit of doing, when, to my surprise, I discovered we had a new visitor and said, "There is a baby skunk eating with the cats." My friend Andrea, to whom I was talking replied, "Oh, of course!" I answered back, "Correction, there are two, no make that three! Wait a minute while I check for more."

There were three baby skunks that had checked in to my "hotel." I guess because of their size, they were able to just slip through the chain-link fence. The other guests at the time, about twenty cats, were not bothered at all by the new visitors, so I decided to keep them until they would be old enough to fend for themselves outdoors. That was easy; getting them out is what proved to be the challenge. Skunks are nocturnal, so I thought it best to plan their release for the night time. All the cats would have to be moved to another area in my basement so as not to escape also. I did this by placing a large portion of tuna fish on a plate, luring them away, knowing they would follow this irresistible scent. I got them all secured and went back to the section where the skunks were, leaving the plate of tuna on the stairs to be taken up later.

To get the skunks to go outside, I laid a trail of cat food, which they had grown very fond of, into the backyard pen and left the back gate open so they would wonder out and return to the wild. It took me so long to get the skunks outside that by the time my mission was accomplished, total darkness had set in. Unfortunately, the light switch for the basement was at the top of the stairs, and I, not being nocturnal, was somehow going to have to crawl through the darkness to get to it. I set off on all fours, groping my way to the stairs and began to climb, totally forgetting the plate of tuna fish that I had left. As luck would have it, guess where I placed my hand, right in the tuna fish! I reached the kitchen feeling quite tired and declared, "I think I'll go to bed."

Two days later a man and his wife came to look at a cat they thought they might adopt. I took them down to the cattery where I had a large cage that I used for viewings. We were talking, as they looked at the cat, when the man said very quietly, "Mrs. Morway, do you realize that there is a very large skunk looking at us?" Apparently we had disturbed his sleep. The nice couple took the cat, and the last thing the man said to me was "This is the first time I have been in close contact with a skunk. What is everybody going on about; he was fine!"

I am not sure how he had gotten in my basement. Maybe the night I had the gate open to release the babies, but now I would have to go through the whole procedure again to get rid of this new guest. The one thing I won't do again is leave a dish of tuna fish on the stairs.

The Prodigal Snail in the Brandy Snifter

O ne day my neighbor's children came home from their beach house with lots of snails — land snails, I think they called them. The only thing I knew was that they looked like snails. The children brought me five as a gift and cautioned me that the snails must be fed apple leaves. They had even given each snail a name.

Not having any suitable container in which to house five snails, I resorted to a large brandy snifter. The children seemed to think this was fine and promptly dispensed their cargo carefully into the glass. One of the little boys handed me a pile of apple leaves and I arranged these inside the glass so the snails could enjoy their first meal in their new home. I then punched holes in a plastic lid from a margarine tub and put it on top so the little creatures would be safe from my curious cats.

All was well for about four weeks. Every day one of the children would stop by after school to bring me some more apple leaves and come inside for a few minutes to visit my new little pets. Each day for four weeks, there were five snails in the brandy snifter happily munching their apple leaves.

At the beginning of the fifth week I noticed that the plastic lid was ajar and that there were only four snails inside the glass. Fearing the worst, I assumed that one of my cats had indulged a craving for escargots and that I would have to break this sad news to my daily visitors. The thought of telling the children that one of my little pets had been eaten was just too much for me. Therefore, the next day I simply pretended not to be at home when the doorbell rang in the late afternoon, waiting until dark to open the door to retrieve my daily delivery of apple leaves. I left a note thanking the children and saying I was sorry to have missed them. My feelings of guilt were strong, but my cowardice was even stronger.

Waking the next day, I went to the kitchen, made a pot of coffee, and took a cup into the living room. As I stood sipping my coffee and staring at the brandy snifter, I decided I had to put an end to my deceptive behavior and reflected on how to break the sad news to the children. While standing there deep in my thoughts, I noticed what appeared to be a smudge on the outside of the glass. I went to get a paper towel from the kitchen and came back to wipe the glass clean. As I bent to do so, I had a wonderful surprise: the smudge moved! My rogue snail was wending his way home. He had missed his apple leaves.

The Psychic Pull

A good friend of mine, who had a beautiful calico cat named Pumpkin, decided to move from Bedford to another town. On moving day, Pumpkin disappeared. My friend looked high and low, as did her neighbors. The following day she returned and looked again, but still to no avail, finally having to leave her cat behind.

This story troubled me. I am not an early riser, but one morning I found myself fully awake and drawn to go and look for Pumpkin. With a scant breakfast I left my house at the unheard-of-hour of 7:00 a.m. All the way to Bedford this insistent feeling urged me on. No sooner had I arrived in the driveway of my friend's old house than a cat, meeting the description of Pumpkin to a tee, appeared before me. I couldn't believe the strong psychic pull between us. I felt as though Pumpkin had called to me that day, and I had responded.

I took Pumpkin home with me, and she and I became fast friends. With my friend's blessing, the cat stayed with me for the rest of her life.

Rosie, the Little Grey Ghost

or feral (undomesticated) cats, I had built a large chain-link cage that helped me to work with them and eventually, hopefully tame them. I would go into the cage daily to clean it and feed the residents. The cage was outside, but connected to a room in the house by a window. This was so these cats could go in and out of the house at will, but would still be apart from my other cats. At this time, I had about eight cats in the cage, including a sweet grey kitten, named Rosie.

During one of my visits, Rosie somehow slipped past me. As dusk approached, I went looking for her. Then I saw her, up a tree. As I couldn't imagine how I'd get her down, I went inside and called a friend, a small, thin woman known for her ability to climb practically anything. By the time she arrived, it was pitch dark, and although Rosie had already descended from the tree, I couldn't corral her. We armed ourselves with a flashlight and a bowl of cat crunchies to shake for bait.

An acre of heavy trees and foliage surround my house. The streetlight was a good distance away, and it was almost impossible to see anything. Fearing that our flashlight would frighten Rosie, my friend and I could do nothing more than set the food dish down and call out softly to Rosie, " Here Kitty, Kitty, Kitty" while straining our eyes to see in the darkness.

Suddenly, we both saw the kitten approaching us. "There she is," we whispered to each other. "Let's wait until she comes to us to pick her up," I said. Just as the kitten reached our feet, I bent down and *poof!*, she disappeared. My friend and I had our arms around each other, jumping up and down, squealing, "We saw her! We saw her!" Yet at this point, we realized that we must have seen a ghost and that we had to give up the search. We went inside, considerably shaken feeling rather foolish.

I never found Rosie, although talking about it later, my friend and I realized that we could never have seen the real kitten anyway, conditions were simply too dark. We remembered that the grey kitten seemed to have had a light of her own.

Since then, I have wondered whether this episode, too, might represent yet another instance of one of my kitties, having died, responding to my "Kitty, Kitty, Kitty" call just to let me know that we are not, after all, so very far from each other.

Munchkin

A friend of mine died and left behind her black male cat named Munchkin. Traumatized by the loss of his mistress and the volume of relatives and strangers going in and out of the house, Munchkin sought refuge under my friend's bed and refused to come out. Kind souls tried to lure him out with treats and toys, but to no avail. I was called in to see whether I could coax the cat out. I was dubious, however, because even though I often frequented my friend's house, I had never actually seen this cat, as he spent most of his time outdoors.

I went over to the house the next day and entered the bedroom. When I spoke to him, he came right out and into my arms, much to my surprise, and to that of everyone else in the room. Hearing him begin to purr, everyone decided he should be mine. This cat had so much affection for me, he wouldn't leave my side. At night he slept on my bed with a few other "family members" — one of whom was a dog. He soon became the dominant male cat in the house, a role he seemed to love. Munchkin was thriving.

Unfortunately, at the time I was in severe pain and in need of knee surgery. And so within two weeks of Munchkin's arrival, I had to be hospitalized. I was always concerned when leaving my animals with caregivers, and was especially worried about Munchkin, since he hadn't been in my house very long. Following the surgery and recovery at the hospital, I was scheduled to spend two weeks in a rehabilitation facility in Woburn, Massachusetts. About three days before I was to leave for the rehab clinic, I began dreaming about Munchkin. Each morning, upon awakening, I thought of him first thing and all through the day. Munchkin's presence became so insistent that I knew I had to go home.

I called the nurse and told her I was leaving. All the hospital staff knew me well enough to realize that if I had my mind set on something, it would happen. They called my daughter-in-law to come get me. When Nancy arrived, the nurse wheeled me to the exit and out to the car. Although still in some pain, I awkwardly climbed into the car, and we set off for home.

On arrival, as I slowly hobbled through the front door, I was greeted by the most wonderful sight. A few caring friends, and all my cats, were in the living room, lounging around on the sofa and chairs. I could only think that Nancy must have alerted them before picking me up. My scruffy little brown dog, Peanut, jumped up on the sofa beside me and licked my face. Looking around I felt very happy to be home. However, in looking more closely, I realized there was a crucial character missing in the room, Munchkin.

Turning to one of my friends who had been caring for my animals, I asked if she knew where Munchkin was. She looked a bit sheepish and admitted that he had crawled under my bed the first night I was in the hospital and hadn't come out since. All of the caregivers' attempts to get him to eat had also failed.

Sighing, I awkwardly got up from the sofa, and leaning heavily on my cane, I made my way slowly to the bedroom. As soon as I crossed the threshold, Munchkin slithered out from beneath the bed and came over to me, rubbing himself against my ankles. The formerly beefy cat was just a shadow of his former self. He had refused to eat the entire time I was gone, an expression of how much he loved and missed me. His physical size might have diminished while I was away, but his heart seemed enormous to me. Munchkin had called me home.

My Hind Leg

Living on an adjacent street was an orange cat who visited occasionally. I'd been warned not to try and make friends with this cat, as he could be vicious. One summer day, I was out in my yard, wearing shorts, and I saw the orange cat. He was looking at me, and from the expression I could see that I should return to the house.

It would have been better for me had I backed away; instead I turned my back on him and tried to sneak slowly to my house. He wasn't about to let me get away. He flew at my backside and bit me severely enough to land me in the emergency room of nearby Emerson Hospital.

When an animal bites you, the ER staff doesn't make you wait. Treating such an injury in a timely manner is very important. I was surrounded by doctors and nurses trying to field all their questions. To this day I wonder what the doctor must have thought when he asked me where I had been bitten, and I responded, "On my hind leg!"

The Man with Too Many Teeth

A woman I knew was moving to Florida, but was unable to take her pair of 14-year-old Maine Coon cats with her. During numerous phone calls, I tried to discourage her from leaving the cats with me. I told her that I feared they wouldn't be able to adjust to being with so many other cats and that because of their ages, they were unlikely to survive the loss of their longtime owner. I recommended that the women find a trusted friend or relative, one with whom the cats were familiar, to take them in.

Some two weeks later, my doorbell rang, and there stood the woman and a man. The woman, holding a carrier containing two beautiful Maine Coon cats, was weeping. The man, standing next to her, wore a smile that was not really a smile, and his teeth displayed a similar falseness.

"I'm sorry," the woman said, "but we are on our way, and he will not let me take the cats with us, nor have I been able to find someone else to take them."

All right, "I replied, "I will take your cats. But I have one request for you. When you get to Florida, I want you to get rid of him."

The women's eyes widened, and her whole expression changed. Although she said nothing, I had the clear impression that I had just given her the suggestion that she needed to take action. Unfortunately for the cats, it came too late. A couple of weeks later I found them curled up together. They had died in their sleep.

Good for Me, Good for My Cats

About nine years ago, Andrea Taylor's teenage daughter, Laura, called the Boston Globe to see if they would be interested in a story about "The Cat Lady of Concord" for their Sunday supplement. They said that they were and sent a nice reporter out to interview me. Before he left Andrea told him that my friends would be giving me a surprise 80th birthday party that Saturday, and since the article would come out on Sunday, it would be safe to use that information in the article. It was a wonderful weekend, what with the surprise party and the article, but little did I know what that article would lead to.

The following Monday morning I received a phone call from a soft spoken gentleman who had read the story all about my experiences with helping cats. He said that he thought I might be just the person to help him out. He was trying to introduce a new cat to his older cat who was not thrilled with the whole idea, and, besides that, he would like to meet me and take me to lunch. I barely hesitated before I said "yes." Afterwards, I called my son who reassured me that it would be okay and said, "Go for it Mother."

I did not know what to expect, and I was a little worried. Had I been too hasty? I watched anxiously for his arrival, and when an attractive tall gentleman with a white beard got out of a Grand Marquis, I said, "Thank you, God."

Off we went to lunch. Both of us were single, neither of us cooked, and we have been lunching ever since. The cats finally relaxed and got along fine, and with my help, we recently added a few more.

About a year ago my son and I decided that living in my little house alone was becoming too much for me; so he arranged for me to move to a new elegant apartment complex in Concord that caters to retired folks. As I was still running the shelter from my house, I was panic-stricken that I might not be able to place my remaining cats in good permanent homes before I moved. Just like me, the cats were elderly, and some needed medication. Who would adopt them? I turned to Richard, for I knew he would have the answer.

Richard's heart is as big as his car — and his car is a huge "sofa on wheels." He is also a big softy. Knowing my plight, he took my shelter cats, one by one, to his house, to see "if it would work out for a while, until we get them homes." By the time my moving day came, all eight cats were at Richard's house in Concord. All eight female, elderly, needy, hungry, temperamental cats were happily establishing territories in his kitchen cupboards, on his living room furniture, and down in the basement den. Richard had a feline harem. With feeding, medicating, litter-cleaning, and belly-rubbing dominating his days, he even found time to take a Reiki class, learning to use this ancient healing ritual to relax and calm his new charges (as well as humans!). Believe me, there is nothing funnier than seeing an elderly gentlemen in a plaid wool shirt and jeans with the cuffs turned up, silently and seriously practicing Reiki on a cat being held in his arms. Richard never complains, and his care is extraordinary. He is a remarkable human being and Annie, Mitzi, Sunshine, Sami, Gladys, Sadie, Lucy, Karina, and I are so lucky to know him.

The Vegetarian Siamese

omeone called me to say that a friend had adopted an 8-week-old Siamese kitten. They were vegetarians and felt that their cat should be also. In addition, their son was allergic to cats, which meant the kitten had to live in the garage. What a life this "lucky" kitten had, fed only vegetarian fare and kept in the garage. The kitten would not touch the vegetables, and my friend watched her getting skinnier and skinnier by the day. In desperation she pleaded with the owners to get some advice from me. They did call me and asked how they could get the cat to eat the vegetables. I told them that cats don't eat vegetables; they are carnivorous. Of course they didn't want to hear that, and I told them if they insisted on sticking to that diet the cat would starve to death.

After hanging up from this phone call, I was troubled and decided to take a cruise by their house. My friend Richard drove as I looked out into the night. I saw the kitten sitting under the light in front of the open garage door. Considering it a lucky break, I jumped out of the car, ran to the kitten and scooped the tiny creature up into my arms. When I picked her up, she felt like bones covered with fur. I couldn't resist. I stole her. It's as simple as that, I knew I had to do the humane thing.

A few weeks later, my friend told me the vegetarians had another kitten. Again they tried to change the cat into an herbivore. Again they failed. My friend watched the same scenario pay out as the new kitty became skin and bones and cried with hunger.

This time, however, the couple must have remembered my words on the telephone. They called me and said that, rather than battling with the cat's nature, they had decided to deliver it to my care. I happily accepted this kitten, and no mention was made by either of us of the first animals' fate.

Floy's Famous Orphanage

One summer, I was feeding my cats in the front middle room of my house. The windows faced the street, and they were wide open, as was my kitchen door. I had been vaguely aware of a car having stopped out front, but it was a very busy street and with all the goings-on, I didn't pay much attention.

When I went back to the kitchen for more cat food, I did a double take. There were three strange cats perched on my kitchen table. At first I wondered whether I might be losing my mind, but then I realized that these were three newcomers. Someone had clearly driven up, and seeing that I was busy had the nerve to simply drop them off. What did they think I ran anyway — an orphanage?

Yes, I guess I did. These poor cats, having been deposited on my kitchen table were too shocked to move. They just sat there dolefully, staring at me with big sad eyes. I gave in, sat down at the table, and began petting them. The familiar cat smells of food, fur and litter seemed to calm them as much as my petting. Soon, my three new orphans were happily blending in with the others.

The Day Geo Died

A 15-year-old gray-and-white cat, Geo, was constantly in the company of Wellington, a large orange tiger cat. I lived on a busy street, but neither had ever left the confines of my woodsy backyard until the day a strange calico cat, a female, wandered through. Geo began following. I called him, and, fortunately, he came back as the other cat went on her way. I brought in both Geo and Wellington in case either got ideas. The next morning, I looked around before letting them out; no other cat was in sight..

Leaving both Geo and Wellington lying contentedly, sunning themselves on the walkway, I went about other things. I checked a half hour later, but they were nowhere to be seen, which was very unusual for those two. I called but received no response. Then, at the end of the driveway, some seventy-five feet away, Wellington appeared. Alone.

Softly, I said "Oh, Wellington, where is Geo?" I knew something had happened. I could not see Wellington's eyes from this distance, just his body. Suddenly, his face came

toward me, and his eyes were large and round and penetrating — just as though he was only a foot in front of me. "Show me," I said simply, and his face receded. Wellington went back into the bushes lining the driveway.

I called a friend, Eleanor, to accompany me, and together we went looking. I knew Geo was dead, but had to see for certain and would not give up until I had found him. Very often when a cat has been hit by a car, they will crawl off to die. Putting Wellington back in the house, we scoured the woods. "Give up," Eleanor advised, as darkness began to fall, but I would not.

Since it was dark, I returned home to get a flashlight to continue the search. There was one more place to check. Eleanor resisted a bit, "Do you have to check every corner of this neighborhood?" I asked her to bear with me. Something told me to go back to a house, two houses beyond mine, that I had checked earlier but hadn't seen anything. There was a deep drop off at the end of the garage which was concealed by bushes. Eleanor said, "Don't go down there. You will fall, Floy." I said "I have to."

I got down over the embankment and pushed aside the bushes. There was my Geo. My search was ended. My friend could not believe how I could have gone so directly to where he lay. I think Geo wanted me to know where he was. I lovingly carried his lifeless body home.

The Great Rabbit Rescue

I learned one day about a rabbit who was kept outside in a cage. From what I'd been told, the rabbit was underfed, given insufficient water, and deprived of loving care. It was a hot summer, and I could imagine the poor creature's misery. I managed to find out the hours when the owners would be at work. During one of these times, I inspected the premises and found the report of negligence to be true: no food, no water. Over the next three days I brought the little creature food and water at the same time, when I knew the owners weren't there.

Much to my surprise, however, on the fourth day, they were waiting for me. Externally, I didn't bat an eyelash: internally, however, I was shaking. I began the conversation, "Are you the owners of this rabbit?" "Yes," the man replied. "And what are you doing trespassing on our property?"

"Well," I said, "This animal is not being properly cared for. I'm willing to give you another chance, but if you don't improve the situation quickly, I'll report you to the authorities."

The woman's voice grew high-pitched, and they demanded that I withdraw from their property immediately. I went home and thought about the situation. I called people I knew who cared about such small pets and whether they would help rescue the rabbit. Their response was resoundingly affirmative. Another sympathetic friend kept me apprised of the rabbit's fate and the times when the owners were likely to be away. I had spies everywhere.

Within days, one of these supporters, a black-shrouded figure with a hood pulled over her eyes, appeared in my driveway. We shared a good laugh and then departed to get the job done. We drove to the "crime scene," and my friend kept the motor running while I swiftly accomplished "the snatch," before we sped off. The rabbit was saved! That afternoon, not unexpectedly, I had a visit from the rabbit's owners. I was ready for them.

"Where is our rabbit?" they demanded

"What?" I asked with a straight face, deserving that year's Academy Award for Best Actress. "Something has happened to your rabbit? I loved that animal!"

"We know you have it. Where is it?"

"Well, come on in, "I responded. "And if you find your rabbit, you can have him. But while you're at it, why don't you check with the little boys who live up the street from your house? They know how mistreated your rabbit was, and maybe they rescued it."

The owners realized there was nothing more they could do as they didn't find the rabbit. In nearby Arlington, Massachusetts, however, a very happy family and a very happy rabbit were enjoying their first night together.

The Christmas Bag Cat

Several years ago two friends, Flo and Irene, and I went Christmas shopping. Around lunchtime we drove to a Friendly's restaurant at the local mall. As we pulled into a parking space and got out of the car, we noticed a female cat just under the car next to ours. She had apparently been run over and killed. Being animal lovers, we could not just leave her there, so we consolidated our purchases into fewer bags, wrapped the poor kitty in festive tissue paper, and gently placed it into one of the now empty Christmas shopping totes, tying it securely shut with some ribbon. We then left the bag on the roof of our car and began walking the short distance toward the restaurant, but we decided that the cat should really be left inside the car.

Turning around to head back for the car, we saw a woman standing by it, looking around furtively. Suddenly, she reached for the brightly decorated bag on the car's roof and made off with what she thought was a treasure. Carrying her find, the woman headed straight for Friendly's. We followed in right after her and took a booth where we could keep an eye on her to see what she would do. We were having a lot of trouble maintaining our dignity.

She could not wait to see what she had just acquired. She quickly untied the ribbon, peeled aside the tissue paper, and took a look inside the bag — then she screamed and fainted dead away in the booth. The restaurant staff rushed over, and one of them called the police, who promptly arrived in time to revive the women and calm her down.

With that, we got up and left to go elsewhere for lunch. Although there was nothing more we could do for the kitty, I have to confess that when we settled down in the car, the humor of the situation suddenly hit us, and we exploded into laughter: That poor woman will never again try to walk off with a "treasure," no matter how tempting it looks.

We also wondered how she would explain the presence of a dead cat in such a nice shopping bag from a local store.

Susie

One day, friends hosting a birthday lunch for me at their home began telling me about a small Shih Tzu, Susie, who lived in their neighborhood, but was being ignored and probably mistreated by her owners. My friends wondered whether I could do something about the situation. Though hesitant, I promised to investigate. The family in question was rumored to be in trouble with the law and was planning on moving shortly. They had several cats in addition to the dog. I had the distinct impression that these animals would be left behind.

Although I knew where the house was, a snowstorm was forecast for that afternoon, and I was a little concerned about being able to get through. Still, I decided that there was no time like the present. I found the house and rang the doorbell. From inside I heard a tiny bark, as if to say, "You finally got here." A couple of teenage boys, each about six feet tall, came to the door. The little dog was at their feet. The boy's mother, sitting on the couch facing the door, didn't even bother to stand or even look up.

As the sun was in my eyes, which tend to tear with bright light, I decided to do a Sarah Bernhardt impression and began crying crocodile tears, claiming that I had just lost a dog exactly like theirs. There was no response. I cranked it up: "I'll pay for her!" I exclaimed. Up came the heads, "How much?"

"Well I have $25 with me." Quickly came the response: "Fine." Inwardly, though, I was amazed. Who would sell their pet for $25 if they cared for it at all?

One of the sons told me that Susie was about 8-years old and had been spayed. That was all I needed to hear. "Come on, baby," I said, and the little dog came right along hopped happily into my car, without hesitation. Susie looked like a great big Brillo pad, sticks and burrs inhabiting her tangled fur, and she smelled something fierce. I drove back to my friends' house and honked the horn. They came to the door, asking, "Did you forget something?"

"I didn't forget anything." I replied. "I have a surprise for you. Is this what you wanted me to get this morning?"

"Oh, you did it!" they screamed. Looking at the dog's deplorable condition, my friends suggested that we take Susie straight to the groomer.

I called Richard, who with my other friends, took Susie to the groomer while I went home to get ready for her arrival. When Susie arrived at my house, she'd been transformed into a clean, happy, sweet-smelling creature. Animals know so much more than we give them credit for. In the light of Susie having barked a single bark of welcome when I came to the door and her having been more than ready to go right with me, I believe that in some sense Susie had been waiting for me.

I hesitated to keep Susie myself, as I'd just recently lost two dogs. I just didn't think I could handle another such devastating loss, so I vowed to find her a good home. I put an ad in the paper and received two responses right away. The first family had another Shih Tzu and thought Susie would make a fine companion. Accordingly, off she went to that home. But the next morning the family called and said, "We're afraid you'll have to come and get her. She clearly doesn't want to be here. She barked all night long and scratched at the door. No one in the house got any sleep. We'd love to keep her, but she's not happy."

The second family, also an excellent prospect, had a wonderfully large yard for Susie to play in. Thus, off she went again. Soon, however, this family called too. This time at 11:30 p.m, to report that Susie was having no part of their home and had been barking continuously. And so I again called my friend Richard, and together we drove over to retrieve her. When we reached the door, she ran to us. Richard cradled her in his arms and took her to the car. Susie immediately nestled herself into the crook of his left arm,

THE CAT LADY OF CONCORD

feeling very secure, a practice she maintained throughout her life. As soon as we reached my house, Susie ran in, hopped up on the bed, and before falling asleep, looked up at me as if to say, "I've won the battle, I'm home for good now."

Susie was with me for four more wonderful years. Unfortunately, she developed an enlarged heart. She had been in failing health for some time, and her ability to breathe had become more and more labored. Moving around was painful for her and she was becoming less and less interested in food. So, with my veterinarian's advice, I decided that the time had finally come. Richard and I, with heavy hearts, put her in her little bed in the back seat of his car. In her healthier days she had insisted on riding on Richard's lap, but lately she had been so lethargic that the bed seemed the best option.

But something must have clicked for her during our ride, because somehow she got herself over into the front seat. She was so happy to be there with Richard, something she hadn't done for weeks. Her renewed energy continued even as we took her into the doctor's office. However, it became evident that this was a momentary surge and that the underlying pain and disability was still much present. We showered her with our love and appreciation as she died. It was absolutely devastating. We mourned her loss for many days. Everything reminded us of her. I kept finding her little cookies everywhere, and I found myself looking for her eager little face as I rounded every corner in my house.

When she had been her healthy self, she would display her tremendous love for Richard every time he came to the house. She recognized the sound of his car, and as he passed by her look-out window, she would begin her crazy happy dance charging around the living room, jumping up on the furniture and around in circles until he came through the door and gave her a little treat and a warm greeting pat. Vanna, my large, white cat took all this excitement in from her perch, usually with a yawn and a stretch turning over to another comfortable position. But one day, not long after Susie had left us, Vanna suddenly came alive, in much the same way Susie had, to the sound of Richard's approach. Never before and never again since, has she displayed the ability or the interest in such antics, but there she was, repeating Susie's greeting for Richard. I believe it was Susie's spirit that got into her to let me know that she was still with us.

Cats
Against the Odds

E ach of the cats that has come into my life has had a story of its own, and sometimes even the names I give them have been a reflection of that story. Some stories are more remarkable than others, but they all have been very memorable to me. They say that cats have nine lives, and I have really come to appreciate the truth in that statement. It still amazes me, though, their resilience against the odds.

One cat, given the name Shivers, was found on a cold rainy day in winter, at the bottom of a dumpster. Suffering from hypothermia, he was more dead than alive. Yet after twenty-four hours of lying on a heating pad in front of a woodstove, and being fed many small helpings of food and liquid, he bounced back and joined the crew. Soon he was fit to be adopted by a nice new family.

There was also Last Chance. Someone was taking her to the vet to be put to sleep just as I was entering the vet's office. I asked her owner what was wrong with this beautiful animal. The lady explained that she was moving and couldn't take the cat. I couldn't believe it — this was a healthy cat, and all she could think of for convenience sake was to have her put down. Needless to say, the cat didn't even make it to the reception desk, hence her name.

Another one, surviving great odds, to come to mind was Herman, a very relaxed cat. He came to me with BB pellets embedded in his hindquarters and a flea collar that had grown into the flesh around his neck. Herman almost didn't make it, but his fortitude brought him through, and due to his old age when I rescued him, I kept him to become a permanent member of my clan.

And then there was Blackjack. Had I not gone to my son's summerhouse and stumbled over a box, Blackjack would have been dead within the hour. When I took him out he was dripping wet and severely dehydrated. I nursed that little fellow for a year with the help of my vet, but, unfortunately, severe damage had been done by that cruel treatment, and our efforts could not fully restore his health. I guess his time was up, but I take comfort in the fact that it was my love that gave him a happy last year.

My New Home

It was my first evening at Newbury Court, and I was exhausted. It had been a long day of moving, and I had done too much; so my legs were red and swollen all the way up to my hips. Since bed was the best place to be, I changed into my evening attire, a comfy three-quarter-length T-shirt with a large cat picture on the front — of course. Before retiring I realized that I wanted to stick a note to my outside front door letting a friend know to knock loudly when she came tomorrow to visit.

As I opened the door my white cat, Vanna, decided to escape, and she shot out into the hall. I stepped out to reach for her, and my front door closed behind me. There I stood in all my glory, locked out. I thought to myself that if ever I was going to have a heart attack, now would be the time.

What should I do? I knew that I was the first occupant on my floor, so knocking on doors wouldn't help. I had noticed a young fellow painting earlier and he had left a closet open with a light on, and I grabbed Vanna, threw her into the

THE CAT LADY OF CONCORD

room, and closed the door. At that point I reckoned the only thing I could do was go down to the office to get a spare key. Remembering my attire, or lack there of, I knew if I ran into anyone, they would probably turn and run the other way.

I got into the elevator and being a little distraught, I pushed the LG button thinking this was the lounge. I was soon to find out that LG meant Lower Garage. I really became upset, so I pushed any button just to get out of there. This took me to the third floor. I then took a deep breath and said to myself, "Let's try 1, Floy!"

Well the elevator opened on the first floor , and there, just opposite the elevator door, was a big comfy chair into which I promptly collapsed. I knew that the desk was occupied but there was a long hallway that I would have to navigate, and at that point I felt I could no longer walk. I called out in my loudest voice "Hello." Nothing happened. I tried it again, and a young workman pushing a large loader finally arrived. He looked at me and the vision he saw left him speechless. I said jokingly "Is that for me?"

He said "Would you like something better?" I nodded, and he said "I will get you a wheelchair."

He went off in search of a wheelchair, and a nice lady came down the hallway asking if someone had called out. I explained my circumstances, and that I needed a key to re-enter my apartment. She told me that she couldn't leave the front desk unattended and that she would have to find someone to relieve her at the desk while she wheeled me home. The workman arrived with the wheelchair and stayed with me until the woman arrived with my key. This all seemed to be taking an eternity, and I looked at the young fellow and said, "She is never coming back, is she?" and we both started to laugh. Finally she came and explained that she had taken a while to locate someone to cover the desk in her absence.

The young worker insisted on coming with us declaring, "I am going with you, because I want to see this through until the very end." When we got upstairs, I opened my door, and then opened the closet door, and Vanna scurried back into our apartment. I thanked them both profusely, and we all chuckled, for I really was a sight to behold.

That night told me that my family had chosen the best retirement facility for me. If those two people who laughed with me and helped me all the way were an example of Newbury Court care, I knew that I had found a good home.

The Last Rescue

On one of my last trips back to my house on Lexington Road in Concord to finish cleaning out my belongings I made a discovery. I was down in the basement in the cattery, and to my amazement I spotted mouse droppings on the floor! In all my years in that house I had never seen any signs of mice, but now that there was no one living there they decided it was safe to run around and show themselves.

I had kept the cages all up on pallets in the cellar in case there was any moisture on the floor; so mice could have been there all along scurrying around totally out of my sight. They probably had developed quite a taste for cat food, too, which was abundantly available. Having the mice there did not bother me, but the knowledge that the house was going to be sold to new owners who just might not be the animal lovers that I am, I had to do something.

Richard and I set out to save the little fellows. We closed all the doors and windows to make sure that the mice could not keep coming in from the outside. We set four Havahart traps in the basement and left for the day. We came back the following day to find mice in all four traps. We picked up the traps and carried them way out into the backyard, past the old doghouse and into the woods, where we released all the mice. Then returning to the basement we set the traps again. This went on until the day we discovered that only one of the traps had mice in it, so we knew that we had them all. This last rescue had amounted to ninety-eight little furry creatures.

Adopt-A-Cat

I n this day and age, most people are familiar with the practice of spaying and neutering pets, and the animal-related terms "No Kill Shelter" and "Humane Education." Some are even familiar with the practice designated by the acronym TNR, (trap, neuter, release) of feral cats. However, when I was a young adult just beginning to realize the plight of homeless animals, there were virtually no support mechanisms in place, except the state affiliates of the ASPCA. Cats were treated as disposable commodities, seldom let indoors, and when kittens were born they were often drowned. There were few veterinarians, and those that were practicing were mostly for large animals such as cows and horses. There were no shelters, and resources for animals were limited. Abandoned animals were a huge, unmanaged problem. Feral cats were in an even worse condition — they were the unseen suffering.

Some kind people fed stray cats, but very few thought about providing permanent safe housing and compassionate placement for stray or abandoned animals. Veterinary care was available only to the lucky few whose owners had enough money and the sense to provide it. As years have passed, many people have become involved in the animal rescue movement, and public support of humane education programs has grown. Today, the quality of life for domestic animals continues to improve in most areas: one exception being the "puppy mill" industry, which is still in great need of attention and intervention on behalf of those poor, abused little creatures.

My early experiences had set the stage for my complete devotion to caring for all animals, particularly cats, thus becoming known, albeit affectionately, as the Cat Lady. My reputation brought me many more cats than I had ever planned. At one point, I had ninety-seven shelter cats and felt pretty much out of control. Some of these creatures were abandoned house cats, some discarded elderly cats, and some feral, untamed cats, which constantly lived in the shadows. Yet, I never lost sight of what each cat needed in terms of food, water and medical attention, and —most important — affection. New arrivals stayed in a large cage for a few days, so as to become acclimated to the environment, and then they joined the group. I had cat beds everywhere, but primarily in the basement. I also had outside pens the cats could access through an open door in the basement. I spent hours grooming, feeding, petting ,inspecting and just plain loving each and every one of these remarkable little creatures. I had a wonderful relationship with my veterinarian, who helped me through any difficult situations. I made sure that every cat I received was seen by my vet and was spayed or neutered and given the necessary vaccinations.

I developed a wonderful network of friends and acquaintances that allowed me to spend many years helping animals. My instinct was to do it all for free, but unfortunately, I didn't have the resources for that. Along the way I decided that it was important to be formally organized as a non-profit organization and registered Adopt-A-Cat as our legal name. I realized that I needed to raise money to do what I wanted to, so I decided to start with a yard sale. Thus what was to become an annual yard sale event began in Littleton forty years ago. It was a great success, growing every year, and it even continued when I moved to Concord. People would collect throughout the year for Adopt-A-Cat yard sales. Our reputation spread and attracted repeat customers as well as repeat donors. In the beginning I made $800 to $1,000 per year (which in those days we considered very good) for my cause. It provided food, litter and medical expenses for my "feline guests" for an entire year.

Another source of monetary support was from the generous financial donations of many other committed animal lovers and very good friends, along with the regular donations of cat bedding and food that went on for many years. I had a great crew of volunteers who came to help feed, cuddle, pat, and play with my furry little charges. They even volunteered to change litter, or as we fondly called it, "scoop poop." In most instances, volunteers were assigned a day of the week and came each week on that day. This system proved remarkably efficient, and also prevented the "burn-out" that sometimes afflicts animal caregivers who see misery on a daily basis. Because of the dedication of these volunteers, my shelter was always clean, tidy, and comfortable for its occupants.

Over the years, there have been many newspaper articles written about my work. These have always generated a lot of interest and made me feel my efforts were truly appreciated. One year there was a community program at the Concord Scout House, and I was invited to bring kittens to it. I brought five or six and was lucky enough to find "good" homes for all of them. Being very selective, I even required a questionnaire to be filled out by the hopeful owners and stipulated visitation rights for myself. I went to many cat shows when we had kittens to place, and this led to many successful adoptions.

You would think my life was hectic enough and that I had plenty of animals to worry about, but I couldn't stand to see animals maltreated. I would often wander around in the summer on very hot days searching for dogs that the owners had left tied up outside with no food or water. I would go right up to the houses and knock on the door or ring the bell summoning the owners. I then would say that I was from the ASPCA, and I had just happened to notice that their poor animal was in need of attention and even perhaps a longer chain. I would let them know that I would check back in half an hour after I had visited a friend.

A good example to me of not being alone in my quest to help others was what one family did when they recognized my need for improved shelter space. I was away on a much needed weekend vacation, leaving the volunteers in charge, and this family rallied together and gave me the prize of a lifetime. When I returned home, I found the old garage doors gone and in their place a wall with new glass windows and a new weather-tight door. Now the room was bright with sunlight, and the space filled with a beautiful warmth — perfect for cats. They could now sit on their perches and look out or just bask in the warm light. I thought Christmas had come early that year.

One very dear friend built me a "cat condo," a structure of layered beds providing comfy nooks to sleep in. Everyone had sleeping quarters. Some liked to sleep together, others by themselves. One cat had to sleep with his paws around another cat or two as far as he could reach.

People from the television show NOVA came to take

pictures one year. They had been to several shelters around and told me that mine were the happiest healthiest looking cats they had seen. I always let people choose the cat they were drawn to. I never worried about how long they stayed with me, and I never put a healthy cat to sleep. The cat that lived the longest with me was 25-years old, a big fluffy happy orange cat.

Under normal circumstances I found homes for about two cats or kittens a week. At the cat shows I could place up to four or five. It seemed like a tiny amount at the time, but looking back, I must have averaged about 200 placements a year. At that rate, over our thirty years, my wonderful volunteers and I have probably placed over 5,000 cats and many dogs.

Now that I am 89-years old, I have had to slow down a bit, but it is really gratifying to know that others will continue with what I began. Adopt-A-Cat, my non-profit organization, will now be known as Adopt-A-Cat of Concord. My friend Andrea Taylor who also has been involved with animal rescue for years has taken up the torch so to speak. She already has a network of cat foster homes to care for homeless animals, but her ultimate goal is to build a state-of-the-art no-kill cat shelter that does not discriminate against any cat, regardless of age, health, or feral status. With respect to my philosophy, she will also be providing outreach to the community in offering humane education, continue humane trapping, low cost spaying/neutering, and adopting cats to loving homes.

The stories in this book are my tribute to the cats and all the other animals in my life, for they have given me so much pleasure. I hope in telling you my stories I inspire you, the reader, to make animals a part of your life also, giving in whatever way you can for in doing so you will get so much back.

"Age is just a state of mind, and if you don't take it too seriously you will last a little longer."

Floy Morway